Best Debt Elimination Plan

Also Available by Keith Dorney

Becoming Financially Independent
book series

Best Debt Elimination Plan *Debt Management Strategies that Get You Out of Debt Quickly and Economically*

A Beginners Guide to Roth IRAs and 401(k)-Type Plans: *Contribution, Conversion, and Withdrawal Strategies for Building Tax-Free Wealth*

DIY Stock and Securities Investing: *Investment Strategies for Building Wealth and Attaining Financial Independence*

Best Debt Elimination Plan

Debt Management Strategies that Get You Out of Debt Quickly and Economically

Keith Dorney CFP® MA

https://keithdorney.com

Disclaimer:

The information contained within this book is not and should not be construed as financial or investment advice: Advice can only be given once an advisor has a deeper understanding of an individual's complete financial situation. The information in this book should be considered of a general educational nature, not financial or investment advice.

This book will educate you with what is hoped to be correct and up-to-date information, but no warranty or promise is made that everything is 100% accurate.

Are you battling high-interest debt? If you answered yes, then I dedicate this book to you. May you have the strength and discipline needed to eliminate it.

Table of Contents

Get Angry

You're not the first person to get themselves into debt. Everyone has made mistakes with money. It's time to lose the guilt and do something about it by implementing the best *Debt Elimination Plan* (page 27).

Why do I call my debt elimination plan the "best" plan? First off, it's free or close to it depending on the media. And it gets you out of debt faster than any other, and in the interim does it for the least amount. That's my definition of best when talking money. I want as many folks as possible to read this potentially life-changing information.

It's important to understand the faster you get out of debt, the less money you'll have to pay. That's good motivation to be even more thrifty, frugal, and clever during your debt elimination period.

Sticking to the best debt elimination plan, which involves changing your spending and savings habits, can be hard. Emotions can help motivate you to find the discipline you'll need to succeed.

If you're not already, get angry at the complicit entities who got you into debt in the first place. I'm not saying this financial mess isn't your fault, but you had a lot of help.

Take credit card companies. They have a long history of ripping off their customers. Tricking you into paying double-digit interest rates and a late fee are their main objectives.

If you've got *credit card debt* (page 41), vow, starting today, to climb out of that high-interest hellhole in the shortest time possible. Then, going forward, never pay them one red cent of interest. Ever!

Many car dealers make more money financing cars than they do selling them. It's their dirty little secret.

They especially appreciate you financing that rapidly depreciating asset with a high-interest rate over a longer time. That makes them even more money. Save big by avoiding the *New Car Smell* (page 50).

The federal government will loan you money for higher education once you reach age 18. No job experience, assets, or income are necessary to qualify.

That's great, but you may be forced into paying high-interest debt to your government for a long, long time. *Federal Student Loans* (page 59), unlike others, are *never* forgiven (with certain limited exceptions).

Don't forget about those payday loan "businesses" out there akin to loan sharks. Then there's our esteemed banking industry's track record, riddled with unwanted opened accounts and fees for seemingly everything.

Love and hate are the two most powerful emotions, the ones most likely to bring about change. Spread and practice love—it's much more fun and productive—but use hate to your advantage when appropriate.

I'm angry that what's contained within these pages is what a lot of folks don't want you to know. Many would rather keep you in debt: It makes them more money. Don't let them keep you down.

Even though you had a lot of help getting into debt, it's you and you alone who must deal with getting out of it. You can't pay someone to do it for you.

Be wary that scammers are behind most get-out-of-debt solicitations. They'll deceive you into giving them money in return for nothing, or worse steal your identity and cause even bigger financial problems.

Even if they could help, your *Spending and Savings Habits* (page 11) are probably what got you into debt in the first place, and they remain the same. It's time to own up to the fact that things must change.

I get excited at the prospect of you eliminating all your unwanted debt. I get even more excited about your *Life After Debt* (page 61). You'll have the opportunity to leverage those newfound spending and saving skills into something spectacular!

Once you're out of debt, redirect the interest you used to pay to others. Invest it towards financial independence, retirement, education, fun, and other pursuits that will make profound, positive differences in your life and those you love. When saved and spent the right way, money can do that.

Changing Your Spending and Savings Habits

Having a clear-cut debt elimination plan greatly increases your chances of success and, as you'll see, is not complicated or hard to implement. It's changing your spending and savings habits that is the hard part. You're up against some formidable obstacles:

- peer and social pressure

- tough economic times

- deceptive advertising

- a "keeping up with the Joneses" mentality

Plan to Succeed

You can overcome these obstacles by deciding how to spend your paychecks beforehand rather than on the fly. Doing a bit of planning now can help you prioritize what's most important in your life. It helps you see the big picture.

Maybe you're not used to spending time on your finances. That's a behavior you'll need to change. I'm not talking about obsessing on the subject. Initially, it may take some time to set things up, but after that, you can pretty much put things on autopilot. There will be some ongoing management duties, but they'll get easier and easier as you get better at them.

Even a little financial planning pays huge dividends.

Planning also helps minimize money spent impulsively on things you don't need. If you're serious about eliminating your debt, sacrifices will have to be made, especially during your debt elimination period, which starts now.

Stop the Bleeding

One assumption I'm making is you're not adding any new debt during your debt elimination period. The last thing you want to do is add to the problem you're trying to make go away.

Another assumption is you have income. If you don't have income, go out and get some. Any amount will help.

During your debt elimination period, if you can somehow make more money, all the better. You'll get out of debt faster and more economically if you can. If you already have a job, think about looking for one that pays more or taking on a second one.

Attack your debt from all angles. Besides trying to increase your income, slash all unnecessary expenses. Eating out, paying for entertainment, taking a vacation, and other activities that cost money need to be put on hold.

Remember, your debt elimination period is a temporary thing. Enduring a little hardship now will be worth it, especially when considering how much money you'll save.

If you have a significant other, buddy up if you aren't already. It's way easier to accomplish any goal when two are working as one versus each independently.

Estimating Income

Take some time to predict your income for the rest of the year, and at the end of the year for the following year. This is a good habit to get into even after you're out of debt.

Estimating your income can be simple if you have one job and are paid a salary, but if you're hourly and/or have multiple jobs, it may be harder.

Break out last year's tax return. Start with past earnings and make any modifications for anticipated future changes. Be sure to include income from all sources. Try and be as accurate as possible with your projections.

I want you to accurately estimate your future income for good reason. From this day forward until your debt is eliminated, a small percentage of each paycheck is to be reserved exclusively for debt elimination.

That debt elimination percentage is to be taken right off the top of every paycheck and applied to your debt elimination plan. The trick is to set that percentage high enough to get out of debt in months, not years, but leave enough left over to live at least somewhat comfortably.

This preliminary planning and subsequent activation of your debt elimination plan is the easy part. Living on what's leftover is where you'll need that emotion and discipline.

Living on What's Left Over

Deciding how your money will be spent before you get it might take some getting used to if you haven't done much planning previously. It's necessary, however, if you want to get out of debt sooner rather than later.

Don't think this means you can't have any fun money to throw around anymore. Just make sure to budget that in. Of course, there must be some give and take, given your income is finite.

That means you must be brutally honest with yourself concerning your spending going forward. Recording how every penny is spent will help.

Expense Gathering Device

It doesn't matter how you do it, just be sure to account for all the different ways you spend money: electronic transfers, debit and ATM transactions, cash expenditures, checks, credit card charges, and everything else. Because your debt elimination percentage is "spent and gone" the day you get paid, it's time to get serious about tracking your expenses.

If you're not tracking your expenses, you're overspending, it's just human nature.

Maybe you've got a system already, but it needs some work, or it's too complicated, or not complicated enough. Tweak it so it's both easy to use and keeps track of everything.

Organize your spending into expense categories. Whether you choose to use three categories or thirty, make sure they account for every penny spent.

My spouse and I like giving our expense categories colorful names. It makes it easier to remember which expense goes where and makes us chuckle when we use them. The name for property tax on our residence is *tick farm tax*. Funds for pet-related expenditures go under *fur babies*, and my wife labeled expenses for my various hobbies as *beast mode*.

Ideally, your device also allows an easy check on expense category balances mid-way through and at the end of the month. That way you'll know if you need to put the brakes on your spending to stay on budget.

You've got lots of choices when it comes to expense-gathering devices.

You can aggregate all your financial accounts in the cloud, automatically update expenditures, and run reports from an app on your smartphone. Mint.com, among others, offers these services.

Maybe you want to secure that sensitive information yourself. There are lots of standalone apps designed to track expenses like Quicken® and AceMoney®.

Know your way around a spreadsheet? Customize it to your liking and track expenses like a pro.

You can go old school with a notebook and pencil too. There is no right or wrong way to do it, just make sure you track every penny.

Standardizing Categories

You need to standardize all your periodic expenses, and to a lesser extent variable expenses, into monthly amounts.

If you're not standardizing periotic expenses, you're just pretending to live on a budget.

Not all your bills are due monthly. Some are due yearly, bi-yearly, or quarterly. Your job is to convert all those bills into monthly ones.

For example, my auto insurance company gives me a discount if I pay the year's premium upfront. I divide the yearly premium by twelve. That's the amount I need to save each month for car insurance.

Some vendors, including insurance companies, may give you the option of a monthly rather than a yearly payment. Choosing that option often is not only more expensive but potentially dangerous.

There can be fees associated with that conversion to convenient monthly payments, and many require you to sign up for automatic payment. Worse, they may insist on a debit transaction, which allows them to debit your checking account whenever they want for whatever amount. Don't give anyone that right other than a trusted loved one.

You've got to be vigilant when considering your payment options. It seems everyone is after your hard-earned money. Seek the lowest cost options and do your own accounting.

Figure out a convenient way to save that extra cash until the bill is due. You can simply leave it there in your checking account: Just be sure you don't spend it. Better yet, transfer it to an interest-bearing account for safekeeping, assuming you're not charged extra for doing so.

Set a budget for all your expense categories. The sum of the category budgets can't exceed what's leftover, of course, so you may have to mess with it a bit to get it right. As with the tick farm tax and auto insurance bill, break down each periodic expense into monthly amounts and save the surpluses until the bill is due.

If you want to be super-accurate with your budget forecasting, standardize your variable expenses too. Variable expenses, like heating and cooling costs, can vary from season to season. Standardize those categories where the variance is greatest.

Once again, beware of vendors who want to do this monthly standardization for you for a fee. As an example, your utility company may offer a fixed monthly payment based on last year's bills, with a once-yearly "true-up" payment or refund. That's fine if they don't charge you extra. Still, you can easily do it yourself.

Once you're done standardizing, there will be fewer financial surprises popping up during the year. You'll find it's easier to track expenses going forward too.

Now, maybe for the first time, if you have money left over at the end of the month, you can spend it with a free conscience knowing you're truly under budget!

Paying Your Bills

Maybe you pay your bills as soon as you get them, or you do it once or twice a month. Whatever works for you is fine, assuming you pay your bills on time.

I recommend not releasing payment to your vendors and creditors until the due date if you can help it. The due date is often weeks away when paying a bill. Keeping money in your account longer can help manage a tight budget. Have the time value of money working for you rather than the folks you're paying.

Two notable exceptions to this rule are credit cards (covered in detail later in *Credit Card Payments*, page 41) and home equity lines of credit. When trying to eliminate these debts, *you want to make your payments as soon as possible.*

I'm a fan of scheduling electronic payments if the vendor allows it. That way you can make your payment on the due date rather than the day you pay the bill.

I am *not* a fan of letting your financial institution have free reign over your checking account. Allowing them to take money out of your account anytime they feel like it is not a good idea. Schedule each payment as it becomes due instead, even though it's a bit more time-consuming.

If you want the convenience of automatic payment, do it on a credit card instead of through your bank account. It's just safer. Check your liability limits and reporting time periods for your checking and credit card accounts: You'll find your checking account liability is much greater.

Also, you really haven't paid that automatic charge on your credit card until you pay your credit card bill, and credit card companies are surprisingly cooperative when disputing charges. That puts you in a much stronger position if there's a problem.

You may shudder at me suggesting you use a credit card to pay certain bills, especially if you've been victimized by credit card companies in the past like I have. I'll explain how to get just the good and none of the bad from your credit cards later in the *Be a Transactor* chapter (page 44).

It helps to assign financial tasks to specific times, like the first of the month, every quarter, the beginning and end of the year, and tax time. If you have a significant other and you're in this together, assign that potentially math-challenged partner of yours some tasks too so they become familiar with the financial goings-on.

Reconciling Your Accounts

There are several financial tasks I recommend you perform as soon as possible:

- Reconciling your bank account

- Reconciling and scheduling payments on credit card accounts

Reconcile all checking and credit card accounts monthly and do it as soon as the statements are available.

Assuming you're accessing statements electronically, your bank statements should be available a day or two after the end of the financial institution's statement period. Credit card statements usually are available a good three weeks before your due date.

There are many worthy reasons to make this a monthly habit:

1. You'll want to find out about identity theft as soon as possible.

2. Through reconciling, your expense gathering device is updated regarding

credit and debit charges, electronic transfers, and checks written.

3. Credit card bills scheduled for payment three weeks in advance help you live on what's left over.

Reconciling is a fancy word for making sure your numbers add up to their numbers. Many apps and websites make it somewhat easier to reconcile by automating the process.

Even if you're not good with numbers, force yourself to reconcile these accounts every month. It may be hard at first; However, as time goes by, all the activities involved with managing your money, including reconciling, get easier. You get better at them the more you do it.

Emergency Reserve Fund

You've probably heard the advice: Save 3 to 6 months of living expenses for those unexpected emergencies. Having an emergency reserve fund is especially important when you're taking your debt elimination percentage right off the top and living on what's left over. It's nice to have a little cushion and peace of mind.

Don't be raiding your emergency reserve for things like a minor car repair or a doctor's visit.

Those types of expenses should be anticipated and budgeted.

How Much is Enough?

Certainly, a worldwide pandemic and its economic consequences qualify as an emergency. After going through that experience, maybe you want to up the amount in your emergency fund some.

Set your emergency reserve fund amount to whatever sum lets you sleep a little bit easier at night.

If you don't have sufficient emergency reserves, it's a good idea to prioritize that as one of your top financial goals to pursue. I've been asked many times which goal to prioritize—a debt elimination goal or an emergency reserve fund.

They are both important, especially if we're talking high-interest debt. On the heels of the pandemic, you might favor funding that emergency reserve first.

On the other hand, you want to start pounding away at that high-interest debt as quickly and with as much money as possible too. I suppose attacking them both at the same time is another option. Pick the strategy that feels right.

Where to Stash It

The nature of an emergency is such that you never know when one might occur. That's why it's important to stash your reserve somewhere that's safe and liquid. A higher-yielding money market or savings account with no fees that carries FDIC insurance would be a good choice.

An account with FDIC insurance gives you an extra layer of protection. The federal government insures protected accounts up to a quarter of a million dollars, or half a million if it's a joint account. The financial institution where you do business probably carries that insurance, but are they paying you a higher interest rate?

You may have to give up some convenience to find one that pays a high interest rate and carries FDIC insurance. Many of them are online without brick-and-mortar locations.

If you're willing to take on slightly more risk in search of a higher rate of return, be on the lookout for new innovative products, like the Vanguard® Ultra-Short Bond ETF.

In my opinion, giving up a little convenience for a higher rate of return is worth it. It may not seem like much, but as you add up a high rate of return here, a lower expense there, as well as money saved on taxes, suddenly you start to notice these positive changes. They make an appreciable difference, especially over time.

Once again, use anger to your advantage. Think of all the times your bank or credit card company duped you into paying them unwarranted fees and charges.

Keep your account and investment fees low and seek out higher rates of return.

Line your pockets with that extra cash instead of helping some rich banker with their Maserati® payment.

Debt Elimination Plan

Sometimes it takes effort and maybe some pain to live on a budget so you can execute your debt elimination plan. You can't hire someone to do that for you, and there's no magic pill you can take to make it all go away.

You've got to take your debt elimination percentage off the top of every paycheck, then be able to live on what's left over. That sounds simple, but if you can do those two things, you've got this debt thing licked.

Debt Elimination Percentage

Your debt elimination percentage is to be taken right off the top of the net amount of money your paycheck generates.

Choose your debt elimination percentage carefully. Once you commit to it, you must have the discipline to stick to it through thick and thin. You've got to defend your debt elimination percentage at all costs!

Until your debt is eliminated, your debt elimination percentage is to be saved every paycheck.

The challenge is setting your debt elimination

percentage high enough to get you out of debt quickly, but reasonable enough to allow for life's necessities.

When I say get out of debt quickly, I'm talking months, not years. The longer you take to pay off those balances, the more money it's going to cost you, which is why you need to eliminate your debt as fast as possible. More than likely, you'll have to make some financial sacrifices to make that happen.

Setting Your Percentage

Ideally, you want your monthly debt elimination percentage to yield at least 5% of the loan balances you're trying to pay off. That's the amount you want to add to the debt's regular payment *each month*. If you can swing that monthly number, you'll be out of debt in no time.

For example, say you have $5,000 in credit card debt and a $10,000 auto loan you want to eliminate.

Your debt elimination percentage should be set high enough to generate $750 per month, which is 5% of $15,000 (15,000 x .05).

Depending on how much debt you're trying to eliminate, that 5% can be a soberingly large number.

If you can't swing 5%, how about 4 1/2% ($675) Or maybe 4% ($600) or 3 1/2% ($525)? If your monthly debt elimination percentage doesn't generate at least 3% ($450) of your total debt, it's going to be a much longer haul.

Getting started is simple. Keep making your "regular payments" for all your debts. Add your debt elimination percentage to the regular payment of your highest-interest debt. Do it every month until your debt is eliminated.

Make sure your creditor understands the purpose of that extra money, which is above and beyond the regular payment. It's to be used to reduce the principal balance that you owe them, not to be held for payments of "future interest and principal payments" or some other nonsensical reason.

Your creditor could try this trick. Just another game they play. Don't fall for it. Make two separate transactions if necessary and check your statement next month to be sure the principal was reduced appropriately.

What's a Regular Payment?

When I say regular payment, I mean whatever payment you've regularly been making to your creditors.

In the case of a student loan, it might be the fixed amount set by the payback option you chose. For a credit card, it could be the minimum payment or a higher amount. Whatever payment you've been making, that's your regular payment.

If you haven't made a payment in a while, make sure you contact your creditor right away. Let them know the good news: You're planning to pay back every penny you owe them. Many creditors are willing to work with you, but it's you who must initiate the conversation.

Be wary of any "deal" your creditor may offer you. Remember, you're negotiating with the enemy here. They're not beneath preying on your desperation.

For example, your creditor might offer you a new regular payment that is lower than your previous one. What they'll keep on the down-low is they extended the term of your loan and probably raised your interest rate too. You'll end up paying lots more money than was owed with the original payment schedule.

At this point, you may have to revisit your budget and debt elimination percentage. It can be a fine line at times trying to balance the two. Just remember, the lower your debt elimination percentage and regular payments, the more expensive and longer time it will take to eliminate your debt.

Writing Your Own List

It's time for you to make your own list of the debt you want to eliminate. You'll need the interest rate of the loan(s). List that first, followed by the regular payment and balance owed:

Interest Rate	Regular Payment	Balance Owed	Creditor

List the interest rate first because if you're eliminating multiple debts, I want you to sort your list, highest to lowest, by interest rate. That means you're going to eliminate the debt with the highest interest rate first, regardless of its size in relation to the others.

Some advocate, when trying to eliminate multiple debts, that the lowest balance debt, not the highest interest debt, should be targeted first. Others say the account that makes you the angriest should be first on your list.

Eliminate your highest interest rate debt before moving on to the next highest.

Psychological reasons aside, I think you need to look at the bottom line here. Going after the account with the highest interest rate first saves you the most money and gets you out of debt faster.

Debt Elimination Example #1

Larry Lots-of-Debt has the following debts he wants to eliminate:

Interest Rate	Regular Payment	Balance Owed	Creditor
15%	$120	$6,000	Debt #1
10%	$100	$4,000	Debt #2
7%	$240	$8,000	Debt #3

Total debt equals $18,000 (6,000+4,000+8,000)

5% of $18,000 is $900 (18,000 x .05)

Assume Larry's bills are due monthly, and his debt elimination percentage generates $800 per month.

$800 is around four and a half percent of his total debt of $18,000, which isn't ideal but still effective. Remember, you want your debt elimination percentage to generate the equivalent of 5% of your total debt if you can swing it.

Debt #1: A $920 payment (the $120 regular

payment plus the $800 generated by his debt elimination percentage) is made to Creditor #1. Regular monthly payments of $100 and $240 continue to be made to creditors #2 and #3 respectively. Do this every month until debt #1 is extinguished. Now turn your attention to debt #2.

Debt #2: A $1,020 payment (regular payments of $120 and $100 made for debts 1 and 2, plus the $800 generated by the debt elimination percentage) is made to creditor #2. The regular monthly payment of $240 is made to creditor #3. Continue until debt #2 is history. Now on to debt #3.

Before moving on, did you notice above how the regular payment for creditor #1 is included in the payment to creditor #2? There are no longer regular payments being made to creditor #1 since that debt has been extinguished, so include it in your payment to creditor #2 to help build momentum.

Debt #3: A $1,260 payment is made to Creditor #3. This payment includes $120, $100, and $240 of regular payments for debts 1 through 3 respectively, plus the $800 generated by the debt elimination percentage. Make this monthly payment to Creditor #3 until Debt #3 is kaput and you're out of debt.

Call this part of the plan a tsunami, avalanche, snowball, pyramid, or some other colorful metaphor if you want. This momentum-building strategy sure wipes out debt in a hurry.

Have you made your own list yet? If you haven't, please do it now. If you have multiple debts you want to eliminate, remember to list them from the highest interest rate on down.

Ways to Increase Percentage

If you're saving for other financial goals in addition to your debt elimination goal, think about suspending those savings in lieu of your debt elimination percentage.

Say you're saving for the down payment on a house, a very worthwhile pursuit. Temporarily stop funding that goal and direct the money instead to your debt elimination percentage. You can set your savings percentage even higher for the house later and catch up quickly once your debt is history.

I'd even suggest suspending your retirement savings temporarily, at least down to your company match (if you're lucky enough to be offered a 401(k)-type plan with a match). Again, the higher the interest rates you're paying, the more desperate you must be.

Look for other ways of increasing that percentage. If you're charitable with your money, whether helping a family member, a local food bank, or a church, it's time to get selfish.

If necessary, have a heart-to-heart with the person or representative of the entity in question. Explain how it's *you* who are currently in dire straits and in need. Again, you can afford to be even more charitable once your unwanted debt is eliminated.

If you get a raise during your debt elimination period, don't even think about it. Keep your expenses fixed and add that surplus to your debt elimination percentage.

Same if you're lucky enough to receive a financial windfall, like an inheritance, bonus, or tax refund. Use it to reduce the principal balance of your highest interest-rate debt.

Debt Elimination Example #2

Sally Spend-a-lot has the following debts she wants to eliminate:

Interest Rate	Regular Payment	Balance Owed	Creditor
24%	$200	$10,000	Payday Loan
12%	$400	$50,000	Auto Loan
5%	$300	$40,000	Student Loan

Total debt equals $100,000 ($10,000+$50,000+$40,000)

5% of $100,000 equals $5,000 (100,000 x .05)

Sally is in a dire credit situation, but it's far from hopeless. Because of her high-interest rates, she needs to take drastic action.

There's no way she can afford to save $5,000 a month on her salary, so it's time to get creative and make some sacrifices.

Let's assume she purchased and financed a new car last year for $70,000. Unfortunately, one year later it's worth just $55,000. 20% first-year depreciation or more is not unusual when purchasing a more expensive car.

Sally needs to act now. In my opinion, she should sell the car before further depreciation causes the market value to plunge below her owed balance. Once that happens, Sally would have to come up with extra money out of her already depleted pocketbook to sell it.

With most car loans, especially those financed with a high interest rate and longer loan term, it's just a matter of time before you're "underwater." Don't go back to the dealership and negotiate a new deal for yet another new car. Get out of this automobile trap now. (More information on auto loans to follow in the *New Car Smell* chapter, page 50.)

Sally could sell the car and buy a decent used car with the leftover $5,000 and eliminate the car debt. Or she could buy a not-as-nice $2,500 car and pay down her payday loan balance with the remaining

$2,500.

The latter would not only eliminate the automobile debt but reduce her $10,000 payday loan balance to $7,500, which is huge. Since Sally's payday loan company charges 24% on her balance daily, she'd begin enjoying significantly lower interest charges immediately.

Sally might even want to consider a principal reduction of the payday loan debt with the remaining $5,000 from the sale of the car, reducing her credit card balance from $10,000 to $5,000. It may be worth temporarily bumming a ride to and from work, considering all the interest charges she'll save.

By eliminating her car loan, Sally has gotten her recommended debt elimination monthly amount, which is 5% of all owed balances, down to $2,500 ($50,000 x .05). That's still a lot but getting closer to what she can afford.

What if Sally can't afford $2,500 per month? Instead of using 5% of her total debt as her targeted monthly amount, she could cut it to 4 1/2% ($2,250), 4% ($2,000), 3 1/2% ($1,750), or even 3% ($1,500). Keep in mind the lower the percentage, the longer her debt elimination period and the more money it will cost her.

Sally must find a way to come up with at least $1,500 per month, preferably more; Otherwise, she's going to be in debt for a long time.

The higher the interest rate on a loan, the more desperate you should be to pay it off.

Making Your Payments

The date you're paid and the due date of the debt you're trying to eliminate rarely align. Hold funds generated by your debt elimination percentage in your account. Send those held funds, along with the regular payment to your creditor by the due date.

When To Pay

Except when making *Credit Card Payments* (page 41) or payments on a *home equity line of credit*, making an early payment does not benefit you in any way. It hinders you. This includes most mortgages, student loans, and car loans.

It's critical to understand that most creditors charge you interest every day, but they only allow you payment once a month, at the end of the pay cycle. You can pay early, but they'll wait until your due date to credit your amortized payment and any extra principal you wish to pay.

If they credited your payment early, that means less interest would be generated on that now lower loan balance, resulting in less revenue for that mega-corporation. That's not going to happen unless they're forced into doing it by law like with credit card companies.

Send your payments to your creditors early if you want. Your creditors will appreciate that immensely because early payments make them more money by putting it to work for them sooner. Personally, that's the last thing I want to do.

As you have probably surmised by now, I'm not fond of most of the financial institutions I deal with. The only thing they care about is making more money off me. I resent that. If they were fairer and more honest (some are), I'd feel much differently.

Hate on your greedy creditors like I do by never giving them their money until the due date. This is much easier to do these days through electronic payment scheduling, which allows payment on a specific date.

That way you can pay on time without the risk of paying late, which costs you big time not only through interest charges and fees but a lower credit score.

Avoid late payments at all costs.

Just as your creditors appreciate early payments, funds held in your account give you more utility, whether through interest earned or a more robust cash flow. Have the time value of money working for you rather than your creditors.

Credit Card Payments

Credit card companies are required by law to credit your balance *on the same day they receive your payment.* Whenever you make a payment, no matter how many times a month you make payments, a separate credit is made against your balance each time. This fact can be used to tremendous advantage when paying off credit card debt.

When paying off credit card debt, make payments as soon as money becomes available rather than waiting for the bill's due date.

Pay as much of your calculated credit card payment as soon as possible, even if it's just a few dollars. Send it electronically so it gets there fast. That early payment will make a huge positive difference in the amount of time and money it takes to pay off your balance.

Debt Elimination Example #3

Samir the Swiper wants to eliminate the following credit card debt:

Interest Rate	Regular Payment	Balance Owed	Creditor
28%	$200	$10,000	Credit Card

Total debt equals $10,000.

5% of $10,000 equals $500 (10,000 x .05).

Samir gets paid $1,200 every two weeks. This month he gets paid on the 10th and the 24th, and his credit card bill is due on the 30th.

Samir made some sacrifices to his budget enabling him to set his debt elimination percentage at 21%. That generates the recommended $500 per month (5% of his outstanding credit card balance).

Following the debt elimination plan explained thus far, Samir would hold the $500 generated by his debt elimination percentage and combine that with his regular payment of $200 for payment on the 30th, his due date. *But this is credit card debt, which calls for a different strategy than the rest of your bills!*

Samir does *not* want to pay his credit card company on the due date like with his other bills if he can help it. Samir should pay as much as possible of that $700 from his first paycheck on the 10th.

By reducing his balance on the 10th, he's saving 20 days of super-high interest charges on the part of the balance he is reducing early. This not only saves Samir a lot of money but shortens his debt elimination period.

If Samir can't afford to pay the entire payment from his first paycheck, he can finish it off on the same day that the second paycheck clears on the 24th. He's still saving 6 days of higher interest charges on an even lower credit card balance versus paying on the due date.

If he can keep up that monthly behavior, Samir can cut the time it takes to pay off his credit card debt roughly in half compared to paying on the due date. Even though Samir is paying the same amount of money ($700) each month, he can greatly accelerate his debt elimination simply by paying early!

Only use this debt elimination strategy for credit cards if you're carrying a balance and being charged interest. Once that balance is paid off and it's just last month's charges you're paying, don't let them have their money until the last possible moment—your due date. They hate it when you do that.

Be a "Transactor"

Credit card companies make a ton of money off folks who carry a balance from month to month on their cards. When I say carrying a balance, I specifically mean you're *not* paying off your balance in full each month and are incurring interest charges.

Credit card companies hardly make anything off customers who pay their entire balance owed by the due date. They must harbor a lot of animosity towards us folks, enough to come up with a derogatory nickname. Trust me, "transactor" is not a term of endearment.

This is where you should conjure up some of that ill will you've been harboring and use it to your advantage. That shouldn't be hard if you've been deceived and ripped off by your credit card company in the past like I have. Be a transactor.

A true transactor never ever incurs *any* interest charges or late fees yet takes full advantage of the rewards of the card, whether it be cash back, miles, or some other perk.

To ensure good transactor status, make sure you

reconcile your credit card statement and schedule your payment as soon as the statement is available. This will ensure your expense-gathering device is up to date, the payment will be made on time, and you can correct any potential errors or identity theft issues sooner rather than later.

Remember, a true transactor, once they're out of credit card debt, schedules their payment on the due date and not a day before. Don't let your credit card company trick you into paying it sooner. That makes your credit card company more money, which is the last thing a good transactor wants. It's the least you can do after all those years of high interest charges, fees, and deception.

As explained in *Credit Card Payments* (page 41), if you're in the process of paying off a credit card balance and being charged interest, *you need to make your payments as soon as possible*. I'm talking about life after debt here, where the full balance is paid every month on the due date and not a day before.

Sweet Revenge

Credit card companies make it so easy for you to pay just the minimum payment on your credit card bill. There it is, prominent on the first page, shaded just right for optimal recognition. It's like a siren's song, enticing you to crash your boat into the rocks.

If you look closer at that first page of your bill, you'll also see information informing you how long it would take to pay off your debt if you just paid the minimum payment each month. You'll see it literally takes *decades*, not months or years.

It takes so long because your credit card company is more than likely charging you double-digit interest every day, and you're only paying off 2% of the debt owed each month with the minimum payment. It's insane how much money that adds up to over time.

Do you think that startling revelation is printed there on the first page of your credit card statement out of the goodness of that mega-corporation's heart? Give me a break.

Government regulators over the years have tried to reel credit card companies in a bit to level the playing field with the consumer. That's one of the many bits of information and services they are required by law to provide you.

Those government regulations unfortunately don't stop them from continuing their despicable practices. Trust me, there are folks staying up late at night brainstorming new ways to trick you into paying more.

I remember in the not-so-distant past, if your due date fell on a non-business day and you scheduled your credit card payment on that due date, you were not only charged a late fee, but interest on the couple of days it took to clean up that mess and resubmit your now higher payment. You were supposed to be smart enough to schedule your payment on a business day before your due date.

Going back in time even further before electronic delivery, you had to mail your check early so they received it by the due date to avoid all those charges. They didn't go by the postmark mind you, but the date they received it. Such arrogance!

Now, I love it when the due date for my credit card bill falls on a weekend or holiday. I take pride in scheduling it then, knowing they can't pull their old tricks.

Improving Your Credit Score

I recommend keeping a credit card or two after you've eliminated all your credit card debt. You might think that's bad advice, like throwing gasoline on a fire for someone who's just recently out of debt.

If you think there's any chance in the future you'll revert to your old habits and carry a balance on a kept credit card, it's best to get rid of them all forever.

There's utility in keeping a credit card or two once you're out of debt, but you must never jeopardize your transactor status.

A credit card not only can help manage your budget and earn you perks but improve your credit score too!

Even though you're paying your credit card company what's owed by the due date and not being charged a penny of interest, it's still considered credit. Since the credit card company is spotting you payment of charges you made this month until next month, it shows up as a positive on your credit reports when you make an on-time payment.

Being a good transactor (page 44) means you want to suck all the good out of your credit card and suffer none of the bad. Besides paying on time and never being charged interest, here are a few more behaviors you want to add to your transactor persona that will help your credit score:

- Never charge more than 45% of your credit

limit on any of your credit card accounts. This is considered overutilization by the credit score algorithm and is a big negative. This is true even though you're paying the balance off every month in full.

- Only keep credit cards that you use regularly. Underutilizing your credit card is also scored a negative, so close those cards you rarely use. If you stick to the utilization limits on your remaining credit card(s), closing one down won't negatively affect your credit score much.

- Stay away from "department store" credit cards. Those are cards that only work with a particular retailer. It's easy to accumulate a lot of them since merchants offer discounts on purchases if you open an account. Best to close them all down. Just having them open hurts your credit score since these types of cards have the highest default rates.

Over time, your good transactor habits will overcome any digressions from the past and your credit score will improve. However, I don't recommend using that high score very often. Certainly, it will come in handy when purchasing real estate, assuring you not only of loan approval but the lowest interest rate too.

Try and pay cash for almost everything else. Your days of carrying a balance on your credit card, getting a payday loan, or even financing an automobile purchase are over.

Don't let the financial entities you deal with keep you down with their deceitful tricks.

New Car Smell

Let's look at some of the pluses and minuses of buying a new vehicle:

New Car Pluses

- New car smell

- No buyer's remorse for at least a week

- Looking super-cool

New Car Minuses

- 10-35% first-year depreciation

- Average 50%-plus depreciation after three years

- Higher taxes and title

- Much higher insurance costs, especially

collision coverage

Financing a Rapidly Depreciating Asset

Suffering wicked depreciation and higher expenses across the board when buying a new car isn't even the worst part. It's the financing where they really get you.

Sometime after you finance that new automobile, the market value of your rapidly depreciating asset and your barely paid-off loan balance will meet. As your vehicle's value continues to plummet from there, so does your ability to sell it. This is called being *underwater* on your loan. The *higher the interest rate* and *longer the loan term*, the faster and deeper you sink.

Don't think you're special because you can get one. Almost anyone can get a car loan. However, the worse your credit score and emptier your pockets the higher interest rate you pay. It doesn't seem fair, but that's the way it is.

Car Financing Example

Vehicle Sales Price	60,000	Amount Financed	45,450.00
Downpayment	15,000	Interest Rate	18%
Additional Charges (1%)	450	Loan Term (months)	60
Amount Financed	45,450	Monthly Payment	1,154.13
Real Vehicle Price	**$83,797.88**	**Total Interest Paid**	**$23,797.88**

In this example, nearly $24,000 extra in interest

charges would be paid over the life of the loan. Even if you have a decent credit score and get a lower 12% rate, you'd still pay over $15,000 in interest.

I hope you see why I recommend paying off high-interest auto and credit card debt before investing. Erasing high-interest debt will no doubt earn you a better return on your money than investing it would.

How Much Should You Spend?

A mentor of mine long ago told me to never spend more than 10% of my yearly income on a car. I violated that edict once, much to my financial detriment, but otherwise, I've stuck to it. It's saved me countless thousands. Sticking to 10% or even 15% enables you to save for a car and pay cash without bankrupting other more important financial goals like financial independence, real estate acquisition, education, and fun.

If cars are your thing and you want a newer car, buy last year's model. You'll still save on that wicked first-year depreciation and enjoy lower insurance, title, and taxes too. Even if it's only slightly used with less than 5,000 miles on it, you'll save thousands versus buying a new one.

The older the car and the more miles, the less

expensive the car. Remember that cars are built to last these days. A reliable piece of transportation can be had for just a few thousand dollars. From my perspective, there are so many better things to spend your money on than a new car.

The automobile trap is a crooked racket and best avoided.

How to Pay Cash

Even if you decide on a more economical mode of transportation, we're still talking about thousands of dollars you'll need for purchase, which you probably don't have lying around. How can you purchase an automobile without financing? First, you need to be realistic as to what is affordable given your income.

Assume you have $20,000 budgeted for a new car. You clear $5,000 a month and can afford to set 10% of your net pay aside for an all-cash car purchase. It would take you 40 months to save $20,000, which is over three years. That's way too long and expensive.

Now let's apply my old mentor's advice. 10% of $60,000 is $6,000. Now you've got your savings period down to just 12 months. A year's worth of savings for your car makes more sense than 3-plus years, and you can buy a fine ride these days with that amount.

Existing Car Loans

What should you do if you're already stuck with one of these wealth-sucking vehicle loans? If your new car smell hasn't worn off yet, I'd sell it and cut your losses, much like Sally Spend-a-lot did in *Debt Elimination Example #2* (page 36). That's assuming the terms of your loan don't make paying it off economically unfeasible.

Unfortunately, there's a lot less regulation when it comes to car loans than mortgages, which means there are some frightful ones floating around out there. Hopefully, you don't have one of them.

Does your loan have a *pre-payment penalty*? If you do, is it for the life of the loan or a shorter time frame? A prepayment penalty penalizes you for paying your loan off early, which is core to my debt-elimination strategy.

In the absence of a pre-payment penalty, is there a *computed interest clause* or other such verbiage committing you to pay all the loan interest originally owed? This despicable loan language lets you pay the loan off early, but you're stuck paying all the interest originally computed per the amortization schedule. If you have one of these, you have my sympathies.

If you're close to or are already underwater on your car loan, it's best to pay the loan off as quickly as possible. If you don't have a prepayment penalty or computed interest clause, you can add extra money to your regular amortized payment per my *Debt Elimination Plan* (page 27).

Old Debt

I believe that if you owe money, you should pay it back. The exception may be old debt.

What I mean by old debt is the creditor to whom you owe money has given up trying to collect from you. They've sold your debt, at pennies on the dollar, to a debt collection agency.

This sale usually takes a long time to happen, after the creditor has tried and tried to collect from you, but in some circumstances, it may happen sooner. Either way, you'll probably know when.

Debt Collection Agencies

It may start with a rudely worded letter. You could be contacted in other ways, often at odd times and in a gruff and insistent manner.

Debt collection agencies have come under fire for their unfair business practices. Regulations have been put in place. Still, outlandish recovery tactics like debt parking, threats of wage garnishment, and calls to friends and family members are still prevalent.

If you're in this situation, consider ignoring the debt collection agency's solicitations and *not* paying. In fact, I'd avoid all communications with debt collection agencies.

There will be consequences if you choose this route. You probably won't be able to get credit for a while, and if you're granted credit, it will be at an outlandishly high-interest rate.

Your spurned creditor could also choose to pursue repayment through the courts. Whether they bring a legal case against you is often money-driven: Is it worth the legal expense given the amount of money loaned and the circumstances?

You don't want to end up in that situation. That's why my best advice is to contact your creditor immediately if you can't make a payment and stay in contact with them until you pay back what's owed.

I'm talking here about spurning communication with debt collection agencies, not the creditor who loaned you the money. You need to realize who you're dealing with, or preferably *not* dealing with.

Find out more about these nefarious practices and your rights at *Nolo.com/legal-encyclopedia/top-five-debt-collector-phone-tactics*.

Another problem with old debts such as those

described, besides the scary debt collectors, is there's a chance that debt may be "reset." By making a payment to a collection agency, this action often resets the clock, and your old debt now becomes a new debt again on your credit reports. That could result in another seven years of negative reporting to the credit bureaus.

By leaving that old debt alone, it should disappear as a negative on your credit reports seven years from the last reportable action. Note that bankruptcies stay on your reports for ten years.

Federal Student Loans

Federal student loans are the exception. They never "go away." The federal government will dog you until the day you die for repayment, eventually garnishing tax refunds and your paychecks to get their money. There are exceptions (*https://studentaid.gov/articles/student-loan-forgiveness*), but they are either not available or unrealistic for most.

With limited exceptions, federal student loans absolutely must be paid back.

Checking Your Credit Reports

That's a good reason to check your credit reports at annualcreditreport.com (*https://www.annualcreditreport.com/index.action*) at least once a year. Unpaid bills you may have forgotten about will show up there. Debts you owe but are unaware of because you moved and never received a bill will also be present. Then you can pay your creditors what you owe and be done with it.

Life After Debt

Imagine the day you get out of debt. Go on, close your eyes for a moment, and imagine you've embraced and implemented the strategies outlined here. After all your hard work, the day has finally come. You've eliminated your unwanted debt. Feels good, doesn't it? What's your next step?

I urge you to reward yourself and restore some of that suspended spending you endured during your debt elimination period. You deserve it. But what about the rest?

Most Important Money

Turn your debt elimination percentage into your prosperity percentage.

Whether it's all your former debt elimination percentage or a fraction thereof, treat your prosperity percentage just like your former debt elimination percentage. Take it right off the top every time you get paid.

Call it your prosperity percentage, saving percentage, or whatever, it's your *most important money*. If distributed and invested thoughtfully, it could bring about a whole lot of good in your life.

This is where things get exciting. Instead of using that money to eliminate your debt, now you're investing those per paycheck sums into customized investment plans for financial independence, retirement, education, or whatever else it is you desire.

Financial Independence

Certainly, financial independence must be on your radar as a financial goal. Being able to do what you want when you want, without having a paycheck hanging over your head is something just about everyone craves.

Getting rid of your unwanted high-interest debt is the first step on your road to financial independence. That's why it's book 1 of my 3-book series *Becoming Financially Independent*. Getting out of debt and staying out of debt is more important than ever in these crazy and unpredictable times.

So, how are you going to spend the extra money you've just freed up? I suggest spending it on something spectacular, something that will make a profound, positive difference for you and your loved ones.

Buying a home that you'll not only enjoy but is

sure to appreciate is a good example. So is retiring when you want with the money you need.

Giving yourself or a loved one the ability to make more money during their lifetime through higher education is an amazing financial goal. So is financing a dream of entrepreneurship.

Can you imagine having the thing you love to do most as your job? That's something to which all of us can aspire.

Ideally, like my examples, most of your financial goals should share the following characteristics:

- Potential to appreciate or enable one to make more money

- Makes profound, positive differences in the lives of you and your loved ones

Try and direct most if not all your most important money to goals such as these. Of course, you'll save for financial goals that don't appreciate or give you the ability to make more money. I'm all for enjoying the moment and cherishing life, which at times costs money.

That's why it's so important to spend some time on your finances. Make plans as to how best to spend your money before you get it. A little financial planning goes a long way. It works way better than deciding on the fly.

I hope you get out of debt faster than you ever thought possible and get back on the road to financial independence in months rather than years. Nothing would make me happier. I'm a teacher at heart, I've found. That's why I love teaching these financial-related topics through my writing, webcasts, and recordings.

I want to wish you the best of luck. Stay debt-free and safe.

###

Summary

Even a little financial planning pays huge dividends.

If you're not tracking your expenses, you're overspending, it's just human nature.

If you're not standardizing periotic expenses, you're just pretending to live on a budget.

Reconcile all checking and credit card accounts monthly and do it as soon as statements are available.

Set your emergency reserve fund amount to whatever sum lets you sleep a little bit easier at night.

Keep your account and investment fees low and seek out higher rates of return.

Until your debt is eliminated, your debt elimination percentage is to be saved every paycheck.

Eliminate your highest interest rate debt before moving on to the next highest.

The higher the interest rate on a loan, the more desperate you should be to pay it off.

Avoid late payments at all costs.

When paying off credit card debt, make payments as soon as money becomes available rather than waiting for the bill's due date.

There's utility in keeping a credit card or two once you're out of debt, but you must never jeopardize your transactor status.

Don't let the financial entities you deal with keep you down with their deceitful tricks.

The automobile trap is a crooked racket and best avoided.

With limited exceptions, federal student loans absolutely must be paid back.

Turn your debt elimination percentage into your prosperity percentage.

About the Author

I want everyone who's in debt to have access to my debt elimination information. Leaving a review at the website where you purchased this paperback will help spread the word. Thank you.

Get to know me better through my free *Best Money Newsletter*. I'll pass along any updates, zone in on a particular money topic, and try and keep it light and breezy. I'll email you just once a month, on the Full Moon. Sign up at https://keithdorney.com.

Once your debt is eliminated, it's time to start your wealth-building with a vengeance. Tackle the remaining books in the *Becoming Financially Independent* series and realize your financial dreams!

After moving on from the NFL, my wife and I settled in Sonoma County, California, where we raised our two kids and still reside. When not writing I enjoy hanging out in the garden and spending time with family and friends.

Detailed Table of Contents